9/01
hole on cover
8-13

WIT

BY

MARGARET EDSON

★

★

DRAMATISTS
PLAY SERVICE
INC.

WIT
Copyright © 1999 (Revised), Margaret Edson
Copyright © 1993, 1999, Margaret Edson

All Rights Reserved

SPECIAL NOTE

Produced in New York City by MCC Theater
(Bernard Telsey and Robert Lupone, Executive Directors;
William Cantler, Associate Director), Long Wharf Theatre, and Daryl Roth,
with Stanley Shopkorn, Robert G. Bartner and Stanley Kaufelt.
Lorie Cowen Levy, Associate Producer; Roy Gabay, General Manager.

New York production originally premiered at Long Wharf Theatre, New Haven, Connecticut.
Doug Hughes, Artistic Director; Michael Ross, Managing Director.

Originally produced by South Coast Repertory,
David Emmes, Producing Artistic Director; Martin Benson, Artistic Director.

SPECIAL NOTE ON COPYRIGHTED MATERIAL
THE RUNAWAY BUNNY by Margaret Wise Brown
Copyright © 1942, Harper & Row, Inc.
Text Copyright © 1970 Renewed, Roberta Brown Rauch
Used by permission of HarperCollins Publishers.

THE DIVINE POEMS by John Donne, edited by Helen Gardner
Used by permission of Oxford University Press.

WIT was produced by MCC Theater, Long Wharf Theatre, and Daryl Roth, with Stanley Shopkorn, Robert G. Bartner, and Stanley Kaufelt, at Union Square Theatre, in New York City, on January 7, 1999. It was directed by Derek Anson Jones; the set design was by Myung Hee Cho; the costume design was by Ilona Somogyi; the lighting design was by Michael Chybowski; the music and sound design were by David Van Tieghem; the wigs were by Paul Huntley; the production manager was Kai Brothers; and the production stage manager was Katherine Lee Boyer. The cast was as follows:

VIVIAN BEARING, PH.D. . . . . Kathleen Chalfant
HARVEY KELEKIAN, M.D., MR. BEARING . . . . Walter Charles
JASON POSNER, M.D. . . . . Alec Phoenix
SUSIE MONAHAN, R.N., B.S.N. . . . . Paula Pizzi
E.M. ASHFORD, D. PHIL. . . . . Helen Stenborg
LAB TECHNICIANS, STUDENTS,
    RESIDENTS . . . . Brian J. Carter,
Daniel Sarnelli,
Alli Steinberg, Lisa Tharps

This production of WIT was originally produced by Long Wharf Theatre (Doug Hughes, Artistic Director; Michael Ross, Managing Director), in New Haven, Connecticut, on October 31, 1997. The production was then produced by MCC (Bernard Telsey and Robert LuPone, Executive Directors; William Cantler, Associate Director), in New York City, on September 17, 1998.

WIT was originally produced by South Coast Repertory, (David Emmes, Producing Artistic Director; Martin Benson, Artistic Director) in Costa Mesa, California, on January 24, 1995. It was directed by Martin Benson; the set design was by Cliff Faulkner; the costume design was by Kay Peebles; the lighting design was by Paulie Jenkins; the music and sound design were by Michael Roth; the production manager was Michael Mora; and the stage manager was Randall K. Lum. The cast was as follows:

VIVIAN BEARING, PH.D . . . . Megan Cole
HARVEY KELEKIAN, M.D., MR. BEARING. . . . . Richard Doyle
JASON POSNER, M.D. . . . . Brian Drillinger
SUSIE MONAHAN, R.N., B.S.N.. . . . . Mary Kay Wulf
E.M. ASHFORD, D. PHIL . . . . Patricia Fraser
LAB TECHNICIANS, STUDENTS,
    RESIDENTS. . . . . Christopher DuVal,
                         Kyle Jones, Stacey L. Porter

AUTHOR'S NOTES

Most of the action, but not all, takes place in a room of the University Hospital Comprehensive Cancer Center. The stage is empty, and furniture is rolled on and off by the technicians.

Jason and Kelekian wear lab coats, but each has a different shirt and tie every time he enters. Susie wears white jeans, white sneakers, and a different blouse each entrance.

There is no break in the action between scenes, but there might be a change in lighting. There is no intermission.

Vivian has a central-venous-access catheter over her left breast, so the IV tubing goes there, not into her arm. The IV pole, with a Port-a-Pump attached, rolls easily on wheels. Every time the IV pole reappears, it has a different configuration of bottles.

CHARACTERS

VIVIAN BEARING, PH.D. — 50; Professor of Seventeenth-Century Poetry at the University

HARVEY KELEKIAN, M.D. — 50; Chief of Medical Oncology, University Hospital

JASON POSNER, M.D. — 28; Clinical Fellow, Medical Oncology Branch

SUSIE MONAHAN, R.N., B.S.N. — 28; Primary Nurse, Cancer Inpatient Unit

E. M. ASHFORD, D.PHIL. — 80; Professor Emerita of English Literature

MR. BEARING — Vivian's father

LAB TECHNICIANS

CLINICAL FELLOWS

STUDENTS

CODE TEAM

The play may be performed with a cast of nine: the four Technicians, Fellows, Students, and Code Team Members should double; Dr. Kelekian and Mr. Bearing should double.

WIT

Vivian Bearing walks on the empty stage pushing her IV pole. She is fifty, tall and very thin, barefoot, and completely bald. She wears two hospital gowns — one tied in the front and one tied in the back — a baseball cap, and a hospital ID bracelet. The house lights are at half strength. Vivian looks out at the audience, sizing them up.

VIVIAN.   *(In false familiarity, waving and nodding to the audience.)* Hi. How are you feeling today? Great. That's just great.

(In her own professorial tone.) This is not my standard greeting, I assure you.

I tend toward something a little more formal, a little less inquisitive, such as, say, "Hello."

But it is the standard greeting here.

There is some debate as to the correct response to this salutation. Should one reply "I feel good," using "feel" as a copulative to link the subject, "I," to its subjective complement, "good"; or "I feel well," modifying with an adverb the subject's state of being?

I don't know. I am a professor of seventeenth-century poetry, specializing in the Holy Sonnets of John Donne.

So I just say, "Fine."

Of course it is not very often that I do feel fine.

I have been asked "How are you feeling today?" while I was throwing up into a plastic washbasin. I have been asked as I was emerging from a four-hour operation with a tube in every orifice, "How are you feeling today?"

I am waiting for the moment when someone asks me this question and I am dead.

7

I'm a little sorry I'll miss that.

It is unfortunate that this remarkable line of inquiry has come to me so late in my career. I could have exploited its feigned solicitude to great advantage: as I was distributing the final examination to the graduate course in seventeenth-century textual criticism — "Hi. How are you feeling today?"

Of course I would not be wearing this costume at the time, so the question's *ironic significance* would not be fully apparent.

As I trust it is now.

Irony is a literary device that will necessarily be deployed to great effect.

I ardently wish this were not so. I would prefer that a play about me be cast in the mythic-heroic-pastoral mode; but the facts, most notably stage-four metastatic ovarian cancer, conspire against that. *The Faerie Queene* this is not.

And I was dismayed to discover that the play would contain elements of ... *humor.*

I have been, at best, an *unwitting* accomplice. *(She pauses.)* It is not my intention to give away the plot; but I think I die at the end.

They've given me less than two hours.

If I were poetically inclined, I might employ a threadbare metaphor — the sands of time slipping through the hour-glass, the two-hour glass.

Now our sands are almost run;
More a little, and then dumb.

Shakespeare. I trust the name is familiar.

At the moment, however, I am disinclined to poetry.

I've got less than two hours. Then: curtain. *(She disconnects herself from the IV pole and shoves it to a crossing technician. The house lights go out. Scene change.)*

I'll never forget the time I found out I had cancer. *(Dr. Harvey Kelekian enters at a big desk piled high with papers.)*
KELEKIAN.
You have cancer.

VIVIAN. *(To audience.)*
See? Unforgettable. It was something of a shock. I had to sit down. *(She plops down.)*

KELEKIAN.
Please sit down. Miss Bearing, you have advanced metastatic ovarian cancer.

VIVIAN.
Go on.

KELEKIAN.
You are a professor, Miss Bearing.

VIVIAN.
Like yourself, Dr. Kelekian.

KELEKIAN.
Well, yes. Now then. You present with a growth that, unfortunately, went undetected in stages one, two, and three. Now it is an insidious adenocarcinoma, which has spread from the primary adnexal mass —

VIVIAN.
"Insidious"?

KELEKIAN.
"Insidious" means undetectable at an —

VIVIAN.
"Insidious" *means* treacherous.

KELEKIAN.
Shall I continue?

VIVIAN.
By all means.

KELEKIAN.	VIVIAN.
Good. In invasive epithelial carcinoma, the most effective treatment modality is a chemotherapeutic agent. We are developing an experimental combination of drugs designed for primary-site ovarian, with a target specificity of stage three —	Insidious. Hmm. Curious word choice. Cancer. Cancel.

"By cancer nature's changing course untrimmed." No — that's not it.

9

and — beyond administration.

Am I going too fast?

(To Kelekian.) No.

Good.

You will be hospitalized as an inpatient for treatment each cycle. You will be on complete intake-and-output measurement for three days after each treatment to monitor kidney function. After the initial eight cycles, you will have another battery of tests.

Must read something about cancer.

Must get some books, articles. Assemble a bibliography.

Is anyone doing research on cancer?

Concentrate.

The antineoplastic will inevitably affect some healthy cells, including those lining the gastro-intestinal tract from the lips to the anus, and the hair follicles. We will of course be relying on your resolve to withstand some of the more pernicious side effects.

Antineoplastic. Anti: against. Neo: new. Plastic. To mold. Shaping. Antineoplastic. Against new shaping.

Hair follicles. My resolve.

"Pernicious" That doesn't seem —

KELEKIAN.
    Miss Bearing?
VIVIAN.
    I beg your pardon?
KELEKIAN.
    Do you have any questions so far?
VIVIAN.
    Please, go on.

KELEKIAN.

Perhaps some of these terms are new. I realize —

VIVIAN.

No, no. Ah. You're being very thorough.

KELEKIAN.

I make a point of it. And I always emphasize it with my students —

VIVIAN.

So do I. "Thoroughness" — I always tell my students, but they are constitutionally averse to painstaking work.

KELEKIAN.

Yours, too.

VIVIAN.

Oh, it's worse every year.

KELEKIAN.

And this is not dermatology, it's medical oncology, for Chrissake.

VIVIAN.

My students read through a text once — once! — and think it's time for a break.

KELEKIAN.

Mine are blind.

VIVIAN.

Well, mine are deaf.

KELEKIAN.   *(Resigned, but warmly.)*

You just have to hope ...

VIVIAN.   *(Not so sure.)*

I suppose. *(Pause.)*

KELEKIAN.

Where were we, Dr. Bearing?

VIVIAN.

I believe I was being thoroughly diagnosed.

KELEKIAN.

Right. Now. The tumor is spreading very quickly, and this treatment is very aggressive. So far, so good?

VIVIAN.

Yes.

KELEKIAN.

Better not teach next semester.

VIVIAN.　*(Indignant.)*

Out of the question.

KELEKIAN.

The first week of each cycle you'll be hospitalized for chemotherapy; the next week you may feel a little tired; the next two weeks'll be fine, relatively. This cycle will repeat eight times, as I said before.

VIVIAN.

Eight months like that?

KELEKIAN.

This treatment is the strongest thing we have to offer you. And, as research, it will make a significant contribution to our knowledge.

VIVIAN.

Knowledge, yes.

KELEKIAN.　*(Giving her a piece of paper.)*

Here is the informed-consent form. Should you agree, you sign there, at the bottom. Is there a family member you want me to explain this to?

VIVIAN.　*(Signing.)*

That won't be necessary.

KELEKIAN.　*(Taking back the paper.)*

Good. The important thing is for you to take the full dose of chemotherapy. There may be times when you'll wish for a lesser dose, due to the side effects. But we've got to go full-force. The experimental phase has got to have the maximum dose to be of any use. Dr. Bearing —

VIVIAN.

Yes?

KELEKIAN.

You must be very tough. Do you think you can be very tough?

VIVIAN.

You needn't worry.

KELEKIAN.

Good. Excellent. *(Kelekian and the desk exit as Vivian stands and walks forward.)*

12

VIVIAN. *(Hesitantly.)*
I should have asked more questions, because I know there's going to be a test.

I have cancer, insidious cancer, with pernicious side effects — No, the *treatment* has pernicious side effects.

I have stage-four metastatic ovarian cancer. There is no stage five. Oh, and I have to be very tough. It appears to be a matter, as the saying goes, of life and death.

I know all about life and death. I am, after all, a scholar of Donne's Holy Sonnets, which explore mortality in greater depth than any other body of work in the English language.

And I know for a fact that I am tough. A demanding professor. Uncompromising. Never one to turn from a challenge. That is why I chose, while a student of the great E. M. Ashford, to study Donne. *(Professor E. M. Ashford, fifty-two, enters, seated at the same desk as Kelekian was. The scene is twenty-eight years ago. Vivian suddenly turns twenty-two, eager and intimidated.)*
Professor Ashford?
E.M.
Do it again.
VIVIAN. *(To audience.)*
It was something of a shock. I had to sit down. *(She plops down.)*
E.M.
Please sit down. Your essay on Holy Sonnet Six, Miss Bearing, is a melodrama, with a veneer of scholarship unworthy of you — to say nothing of Donne. Do it again.
VIVIAN.
I, ah ...
E.M.
You must begin with a text, Miss Bearing, not with a feeling.

Death be not proud, though some have called thee
Mighty and dreadfull, for, thou art not soe.

You have entirely missed the point of the poem, because, I must tell you, you have used an edition of the text that is inauthentically punctuated. In the Gardner edition —

13

VIVIAN.

That edition was checked out of the library —

E.M.

Miss Bearing!

VIVIAN.

Sorry.

E.M.

You take this too lightly, Miss Bearing. This is Metaphysical Poetry, not The Modern Novel. The standards of scholarship and critical reading which one would apply to any other text are simply insufficient. The effort must be total for the results to be meaningful. Do you think the punctuation of the last line of this sonnet is merely an insignificant detail?

The sonnet begins with a valiant struggle with death, calling on all the forces of intellect and drama to vanquish the enemy. But it is ultimately about overcoming the seemingly insuperable barriers separating life, death, and eternal life.

In the edition you chose, this profoundly simple meaning is sacrificed to hysterical punctuation:

And Death — *capital D* — shall be no more — *semicolon!*
Death — *capital D* — *comma* — thou shalt die — *ex-clama-tion point!*

If you go in for this sort of thing, I suggest you take up Shakespeare.

Gardner's edition of the Holy Sonnets returns to the Westmoreland manuscript source of 1610 — not for senti-mental reasons, I assure you, but because Helen Gardner is a *scholar.* It reads:

And death shall be no more, *comma,* Death thou shalt die.

(As she recites this line, she makes a little gesture at the comma.)

Nothing but a breath — a comma — separates life from life everlasting. It is very simple really. With the original punc-tuation restored, death is no longer something to act out on a stage, with exclamation points. It's a comma, a pause.

This way, the *uncompromising* way, one learns something from this poem, wouldn't you say? Life, death. Soul, God. Past, present. Not insuperable barriers, not semicolons, just a comma.

VIVIAN.

Life, death ... I see. *(Standing.)* It's a metaphysical conceit. It's wit! I'll go back to the library and rewrite the paper —

E.M. *(Standing, emphatically.)*

It is *not wit*, Miss Bearing. It is truth. *(Walking around the desk to her.)* The paper's not the point.

VIVIAN.

It isn't?

E.M. *(Tenderly.)*

Vivian. You're a bright young woman. Use your intelligence. Don't go back to the library. Go out. Enjoy yourself with your friends. Hmm? *(Vivian walks away. E.M. slides off.)*

VIVIAN. *(As she gradually returns to the hospital.)*

I, ah, went outside. The sun was very bright. I, ah, walked around, past the ... There were students on the lawn, talking about nothing, laughing. The insuperable barrier between one thing and another is ... just a comma? Simple human truth, uncompromising scholarly standards? They're *connected*? I just couldn't ...

I went back to the library.

Anyway.

All right. Significant contribution to knowledge.

Eight cycles of chemotherapy. Give me the full dose, the full dose every time. *(Scene change. In a burst of activity, the hospital scene is created.)*

The attention was flattering. For the first five minutes. Now I know how poems feel. *(Susie Monahan, Vivian's primary nurse, gives Vivian her chart, then puts her in a wheelchair and takes her to her first appointment: chest X-ray. This and all other diagnostic tests are suggested by light and sound.)*

TECHNICIAN 1.

Name.

VIVIAN.

My name? Vivian Bearing.

15

TECHNICIAN 1.

Huh?

VIVIAN.

Bearing. B-E-A-R-I-N-G. Vivian. V-I-V-I-A-N.

TECHNICIAN 1.

Doctor.

VIVIAN.

Yes, I have a Ph.D.

TECHNICIAN 1.

Your doctor.

VIVIAN.

Oh. Dr. Harvey Kelekian. *(Technician 1 positions her so that she is leaning forward and embracing the metal plate, then steps offstage.)* I am a doctor of philosophy —

TECHNICIAN 1. *(From offstage.)*

Take a deep breath, and hold it. *(Pause, with light and sound.)* Okay.

VIVIAN.

— a scholar of seventeenth-century poetry.

TECHNICIAN 1. *(From offstage.)*

Turn sideways, arms behind your head, and hold it. *(Pause.)* Okay.

VIVIAN.

I have made an immeasurable contribution to the discipline of English literature. *(Technician 1 returns and puts her in the wheelchair.)* I am, in short, a force. *(Technician 1 rolls her to upper GI series, where Technician 2 picks up.)*

TECHNICIAN 2.

Name.

VIVIAN.

Lucy, Countess of Bedford.

TECHNICIAN 2. *(Checking a printout.)*

I don't see it here.

VIVIAN.

My name is Vivian Bearing. B-E-A-R-I-N-G. Dr. Kelekian is my doctor.

TECHNICIAN 2.

Okay. Lie down. *(Technician 2 positions her on a stretcher and leaves. Light and sound suggest the filming.)*

VIVIAN.

After an outstanding undergraduate career, I studied with Professor E. M. Ashford for three years, during which time I learned by instruction and example what it means to be a scholar of distinction.

As her research fellow, my principal task was the alphabetizing of index cards for Ashford's monumental critical edition of Donne's *Devotions upon Emergent Occasions. (During the procedure, another Technician takes the wheelchair away.)*

I am thanked in the preface: "Miss Vivian Bearing for her able assistance."

My dissertation, "Ejaculations in Seventeenth-Century Manuscript and Printed Editions of the Holy Sonnets: A Comparison," was revised for publication in the *Journal of English Texts,* a very prestigious venue for a first appearance.

TECHNICIAN 2.

Where's your wheelchair?

VIVIAN.

I do not know. I was busy just now.

TECHNICIAN 2.

Well, how are you going to get out of here?

VIVIAN.

Well, I do not know. Perhaps you would like me to stay.

TECHNICIAN 2.

I guess I got to go find you a chair.

VIVIAN. *(Sarcastically.)*

Don't inconvenience yourself on my behalf. *(Technician 2 leaves to get a wheelchair.)*

My second article, a classic explication of Donne's sonnet "Death be not proud," was published in *Critical Discourse.*

The success of the essay prompted the University Press to solicit a volume on the twelve Holy Sonnets in the 1633 edition, which I produced in the remarkably short span of three years. My book, entitled *Made Cunningly,* remains an immense success, in paper as well as cloth.

In it, I devote one chapter to a thorough examination of each sonnet, discussing every word in extensive detail. *(Technician 2 returns with a wheelchair.)*

TECHNICIAN 2.

Here.

VIVIAN.

I summarize previous critical interpretations of the text and offer my own analysis. It is exhaustive. *(Technician 2 deposits her at CT scan.)* Bearing. B-E-A-R-I-N-G. Kelekian. *(Technician 3 has Vivian lie down on a metal stretcher. Light and sound suggest the procedure.)*

TECHNICIAN 3.

Here. Hold still.

VIVIAN.

For how long?

TECHNICIAN 3.

Just a little while. *(Technician 3 leaves. Silence.)*

VIVIAN.

The scholarly study of poetic texts requires a capacity for scrupulously detailed examination, particularly the poetry of John Donne.

The salient characteristic of the poems is wit: "Itchy outbreaks of far-fetched wit," as Donne himself said.

To the common reader — that is to say, the undergraduate with a B-plus or better average — wit provides an invaluable exercise for sharpening the mental faculties, for stimulating the flash of comprehension that can only follow hours of exacting and seemingly pointless scrutiny. *(Technician 3 puts Vivian back in the wheelchair and wheels her toward the unit. Partway, Technician 3 gives the chair a shove and Susie takes over. Susie rolls Vivian to the exam room.)*

To the scholar, to the mind comprehensively trained in the subtleties of seventeenth-century vocabulary, versification, and theological, historical, geographical, political, and mythological allusions, Donne's wit is ... a way to see how good you really are.

After twenty years, I can say with confidence, no one is quite as good as I. *(By now, Susie has helped Vivian sit on the exam table. Dr. Jason Posner, clinical fellow, stands in the doorway.)*

JASON.

Ah, Susie?

SUSIE.

Oh, hi.

JASON.

Ready when you are.

SUSIE.

Okay. Go ahead. Ms. Bearing, this is Jason Posner. He's going to do your history, ask you a bunch of questions. He's Dr. Kelekian's fellow. *(Susie is busy in the room, setting up for the exam.)*

JASON.

Hi, Professor Bearing. I'm Dr. Posner, clinical fellow in the medical oncology branch, working with Dr. Kelekian.

Professor Bearing, I, ah, I was an undergraduate at the U. I took your course in seventeenth-century poetry.

VIVIAN.

You did?

JASON.

Yes. I thought it was excellent.

VIVIAN.

Thank you. Were you an English major?

JASON.

No. Biochemistry. But you can't get into medical school unless you're well-rounded. And I made a bet with myself that I could get an A in the three hardest courses on campus.

SUSIE.

Howdjya do, Jace?

JASON.

Success.

VIVIAN. *(Doubtful.)*

Really?

JASON.

A minus. It was a very tough course. *(To Susie.)* I'll call you.

19

SUSIE.

Okay. *(She leaves.)*

JASON.

I'll just pull this over. *(He gets a little stool on wheels.)* Get the proxemics right here. There. *(Nervously.)* Good. Now. I'm going to be taking your history. It's a medical interview, and then I give you an exam.

VIVIAN.

I believe Dr. Kelekian has already done that.

JASON.

Well, I know, but Dr. Kelekian wants me to do it, too. Now. I'll be taking a few notes as we go along.

VIVIAN.

Very well.

JASON.

Okay. Let's get started. How are you feeling today?

VIVIAN.

Fine, thank you.

JASON.

Good. How is your general health?

VIVIAN.

Fine.

JASON.

Excellent. Okay. We know you are an academic.

VIVIAN.

Yes, we've established that.

JASON.

So we don't need to talk about your interesting work.

VIVIAN.

No. *(The following questions and answers go extremely quickly.)*

JASON.

How old are you?

VIVIAN.

Fifty.

JASON.

Are you married?

VIVIAN.

No.

JASON.

Are your parents living?

VIVIAN.

No.

JASON.

How and when did they die?

VIVIAN.

My father, suddenly, when I was twenty, of a heart attack. My mother, slowly, when I was forty-one and forty-two, of cancer. Breast cancer.

JASON.

Cancer?

VIVIAN.

Breast cancer.

JASON.

I see. Any siblings?

VIVIAN.

No.

JASON.

Do you have any questions so far?

VIVIAN.

Not so far.

JASON.

Well, that about does it for your life history.

VIVIAN.

Yes, that's all there is to my life history.

JASON.

Now I'm going to ask you about your past medical history. Have you ever been hospitalized?

VIVIAN.

I had my tonsils out when I was eight.

JASON.

Have you ever been pregnant?

VIVIAN.

No.

JASON.

Ever had heart murmurs? High blood pressure?

VIVIAN.
No.
JASON.
Stomach, liver, kidney problems?
VIVIAN.
No.
JASON.
Venereal diseases? Uterine infections?
VIVIAN.
No.
JASON.
Thyroid, diabetes, cancer?
VIVIAN.
No — cancer, yes.
JASON.
When?
VIVIAN.
Now.
JASON.
Well, not including now.
VIVIAN.
In that case, no.
JASON.
Okay. Clinical depression? Nervous breakdowns? Suicide
attempts?
VIVIAN.
No.
JASON.
Do you smoke?
VIVIAN.
No.
JASON.
Ethanol?
VIVIAN.
I'm sorry?
JASON.
Alcohol.

VIVIAN.

Oh. Ethanol. Yes, I drink wine.

JASON.

How much? How often?

VIVIAN.

A glass with dinner occasionally. And perhaps a Scotch every now and then.

JASON.

Do you use substances?

VIVIAN.

Such as.

JASON.

Marijuana, cocaine, crack cocaine, PCP, ecstasy, poppers —

VIVIAN.

No.

JASON.

Do you drink caffeinated beverages?

VIVIAN.

Oh, yes!

JASON.

Which ones?

VIVIAN.

Coffee. A few cups a day.

JASON.

How many?

VIVIAN.

Two ... to six. But I really don't think that's immoderate —

JASON.

How often do you undergo routine medical checkups?

VIVIAN.

Well, not as often as I should, probably, but I've felt fine, I really have.

JASON.

So the answer is?

VIVIAN.

Every three to ... five years.

JASON.

What do you do for exercise?

VIVIAN.

Pace.

JASON.

Are you having sexual relations?

VIVIAN.

Not at the moment.

JASON.

Are you pre- or post-menopausal?

VIVIAN.

Pre.

JASON.

When was the first day of your last period?

VIVIAN.

Ah, ten days — two weeks ago.

JASON.

Okay. When did you first notice your present complaint?

VIVIAN.

This time, now?

JASON.

Yes.

VIVIAN.

Oh, about four months ago. I felt a pain in my stomach, in my abdomen, like a cramp, but not the same.

JASON.

How did it feel?

VIVIAN.

Like a cramp.

JASON.

But not the same?

VIVIAN.

No, duller, and stronger. I can't describe it.

JASON.

What came next?

VIVIAN.

Well, I just, I don't know, I started noticing my body, little things. I would be teaching, and feel a sharp pain.

JASON.

What kind of pain?

VIVIAN.

Sharp, and sudden. Then it would go away. Or I would be tired. Exhausted. I was working on a major project, the article on John Donne for *The Oxford Encyclopedia of English Literature*. It was a great honor. But I had a very strict deadline.

JASON.

So you would say you were under stress?

VIVIAN.

It wasn't so much more stress than usual, I just couldn't withstand it this time. I don't know.

JASON.

So?

VIVIAN.

So I went to Dr. Chin, my gynecologist, after I had turned in the article, and explained all this. She examined me, and sent me to Jefferson the internist, and he sent me to Kelekian because he thought I might have a tumor.

JASON.

And that's it?

VIVIAN.

Till now.

JASON.

Hmmm. Well, that's very interesting. *(Nervous pause.)*

Well, I guess I'll start the examination. It'll only take a few minutes. Why don't you, um, sort of lie back, and — oh — relax. *(He helps her lie back on the table, raises the stirrups out of the table, raises her legs and puts them in the stirrups, and puts a paper sheet over her.)*

Be very relaxed. This won't hurt. Let me get this sheet. Okay. Just stay calm. Okay. Put your feet in these stirrups. Okay. Just. There. Okay? Now. Oh, I have to go get Susie. Got to have a girl here. Some crazy clinical rule. Um. I'll be right back. Don't move. *(Jason leaves. Long pause. He is seen walking quickly back and forth in the hall, and calling Susie's name as he goes by.)*

VIVIAN. *(To herself.)*

I wish I had given him an A. *(Silence.)*

Two times one is two. Two times two is four.

Two times three is six.
Um.
Oh.

Death be not proud, though some have called thee
Mighty and dreadfull, for, thou art not soe,
For, those, whom thou think'st, thou dost overthrow,
Die not, poore death, nor yet canst thou kill mee; ...

JASON.   *(In the hallway.)*
　Has anybody seen Susie?
VIVIAN.   *(Losing her place for a second.)*
　Ah.

Thou'art slave to Fate, chance, kings, and desperate men,
And dost with poyson, warre, and sicknesse dwell,
And poppie,' or charmes can make us sleepe as well,
And better than thy stroake; why swell'st thou then?

JASON.   *(In the hallway.)*
　She was here just a minute ago.
VIVIAN.

One short sleepe past, wee wake eternally,
And death shall be no more — *comma* — Death thou shalt
　die.

(Jason and Susie return.)
JASON.
　Okay. Here's everything. Okay.
SUSIE.
　What is this? Why did you leave her —
JASON.   *(To Susie.)*
　I had to find you. Now, come on. *(To Vivian.)* We're ready,
Professor Bearing. *(To himself, as he puts on exam gloves.)* Get
these on. Okay. Just lift this up. Ooh. Okay. *(As much to himself
as to her.)* Just relax. *(He begins the pelvic exam, with one hand on*

her abdomen and the other inside her, looking blankly at the ceiling as he feels around.) Okay. *(Silence.)* Susie, isn't that interesting, that I had Professor Bearing.

SUSIE.

Yeah. I wish I had taken some literature. I don't know anything about poetry.

JASON. *(Trying to be casual.)*

Professor Bearing was very highly regarded on campus. It looked very good on my transcript that I had taken her course. *(Silence.)* They even asked me about it in my interview for med school — *(He feels the mass and does a double take.)* Jesus! *(Tense silence. He is amazed and fascinated.)*

SUSIE.

What?

VIVIAN.

What?

JASON.

Um. *(He tries for composure.)* Yeah. I survived Bearing's course. No problem. Heh. *(Silence.)* Yeah, John Donne, those metaphysical poets, that metaphysical wit. Hardest poetry in the English department. Like to see them try biochemistry. *(Silence.)* Okay. We're about done. Okay. That's it. Okay, Professor Bearing. Let's take your feet out, there. *(He takes off his gloves and throws them away.)* Okay. I gotta go. I gotta go. *(Jason quickly leaves. Vivian slowly gets up from this scene and walks stiffly away. Susie cleans up the exam room and exits. Scene change.)*

VIVIAN. *(Walking D. to audience.)*

That ... was ... hard. That ... was ...

One thing can be said for an eight-month course of cancer treatment: it is highly educational. I am learning to suffer.

Yes, it is mildly uncomfortable to have an electrocardiogram, but the ... agony ... of a proctosigmoidoscopy sweeps it from memory. Yes, it was embarrassing to have to wear a nightgown all day long — two nightgowns! — but that seemed like a positive privilege compared to watching myself go bald. Yes, having a former student give me a pelvic exam was thoroughly degrading — and I use the term deliberately — but I could not have imagined the depths of humiliation that —

Oh, God — *(Vivian runs across the stage to her hospital room, dives onto the bed, and throws up into a large plastic washbasin.)*

Oh, God.

Oh. Oh. *(She lies slumped on the bed, fastened to the IV, which now includes a small bottle with a bright orange label.)*

Oh, God.

It can't be.

(Silence.)

Oh, God.

Please.

Steady. Steady.

(Silence)

Oh —

Oh, no! *(She throws up again, moans, and retches in agony.)*

Oh, God.

What's left?

I haven't eaten in two days.

What's left to puke?

(Silence.)

You may remark that my vocabulary has taken a turn for the Anglo-Saxon.

God, I'm going to barf my brains out.

(She begins to relax.) If I actually did barf my brains out, it would be a great loss to my discipline. Of course, not a few of my colleagues would be relieved. To say nothing of my students.

It's not that I'm controversial. Just uncompromising. Ooh — *(She lunges for the basin. Nothing.)* Oh. *(Silence.)* False alarm. If the word went round that Vivian Bearing had barfed her brains out ...

Well, first my colleagues, most of whom are my former students, would scramble madly for my position. Then their consciences would flare up, so to honor *my* memory they would put together a collection of *their* essays about John

28

Donne. The volume would begin with a warm introduction, capturing my most endearing qualities. It would be short. But sweet.

Published *and* perished.

Now, watch this. I have to ring the bell *(She presses the button on the bed.)* to get someone to come and measure this emesis, and record the amount on a chart of my intake and output. This counts as output. *(Susie enters.)*

SUSIE. *(Brightly.)*

How you doing, Ms. Bearing? You having some nausea?

VIVIAN. *(Weakly.)*

Uhh, yes.

SUSIE.

Why don't I take that? Here.

VIVIAN.

It's about 300 cc's.

SUSIE.

That all?

VIVIAN.

It was very hard work. *(Susie takes the basin to the bathroom and rinses it.)*

SUSIE.

Yup. Three hundred. Good guess. *(She marks the graph.)* Okay. Anything else I can get for you? Some Jell-O or anything?

VIVIAN.

Thank you, no.

SUSIE.

You okay all by yourself here?

VIVIAN.

Yes.

SUSIE.

You're not having a lot of visitors, are you?

VIVIAN. *(Correcting.)*

None, to be precise.

SUSIE.

Yeah, I didn't think so. Is there somebody you want me to call for you?

VIVIAN.

That won't be necessary.

SUSIE.

Well, I'll just pop my head in every once in a while to see how you're coming along. Kelekian and the fellows should be in soon. *(She touches Vivian's arm.)* If there's anything you need, you just ring.

VIVIAN. *(Uncomfortable with kindness.)*

Thank you.

SUSIE.

Okay. Just call. *(Susie disconnects the IV bottle with the orange label and takes it with her as she leaves. Vivian lies still. Silence. Scene change.)*

VIVIAN.

In this dramatic structure you will see the most interesting aspects of my tenure as an inpatient receiving experimental chemotherapy for advanced metastatic ovarian cancer.

But as I am a *scholar* before ... an impresario, I feel obliged to document what it is like here most of the time, between the dramatic climaxes. Between the spectacles.

In truth, it is like this: *(She ceremoniously lies back and stares at the ceiling.)*

You cannot imagine how time ... can be ... so still.

It hangs. It weighs. And yet there is so little of it.

It goes so slowly, and yet it is so scarce. *(Pause.)*

If I were writing this scene, it would last a full fifteen minutes. I would lie here, and you would sit there. *(She looks at the audience, daring them.)*

Not to worry. Brevity is the soul of wit.

But if you think eight months of cancer treatment is tedious for the *audience*, consider how it feels to play my part.

All right. All right. It is Friday morning: Grand Rounds. *(Loudly, giving a cue.)* Action. *(Kelekian enters, followed by Jason and four other Fellows.)*

KELEKIAN.

Dr. Bearing.

VIVIAN.

Dr. Kelekian.

KELEKIAN.

Jason. *(Jason moves to the front of the group.)*

JASON.

Professor Bearing. How are you feeling today?

VIVIAN.

Fine.

JASON.

That's great. That's just great. *(He takes a sheet and carefully covers her legs and groin, then pulls up her gown to reveal her entire abdomen. He is barely audible, but his gestures are clear.)*

VIVIAN.

"Grand Rounds."

The term is theirs. Not "Grand" in the traditional sense of sweeping or magnificent. Not "Rounds" as in a musical canon, or a *round* of applause (though either would be refreshing at this point). Here, "Rounds" seems to signify darting *around* the main issue ... which I suppose would be the struggle for life ... *my* life ... with heated discussions of *side* effects, *other* complaints, *additional* treatments.

Grand Rounds is not Grand Opera. But compared to lying here, it is positively *dramatic.*

JASON.

Very late detection. Staged as a four upon admission. Hexametho-phosphacil with Vinplatin to potentiate. Hex at 300 mg. per meter squared, Vin at 100. Today is cycle two, day three. Both cycles at the *full dose. (The Fellows are impressed.)* The primary site is — here, *(He puts his finger on the spot on her abdomen.)* behind the left ovary. Metastases are suspected in the peritoneal cavity — here. And — here. *(He touches those spots.)*

Full lymphatic involve-ment. *(He moves his hands*

31

Full of subservience, hierarchy, gratuitous displays, sublimated rivalries — I feel right at home. It is just like a graduate seminar.

With one important difference: in Grand Rounds, *they* read *me* like a book. Once I did the teaching; now I am taught. This is much easier. I just hold still and look cancerous. It requires less acting every time.

Excellent command of details

over her entire body.)

At the time of first-look surgery, a significant part of the tumor was de-bulked, mostly in this area — *here.* *(He points to each organ, poking her abdomen.)* Left, right ovaries. Fallopian tubes. Uterus. All out.

Evidence of primary-site shrinkage. Shrinking in metastatic tumors has not been documented. Primary mass frankly palpable in pelvic exam, frankly, all through here — *here. (Some Fellows reach and press where he is pointing.)*

KELEKIAN.
    Excellent command of details.
VIVIAN.   *(To herself.)*
    I taught him, you know —
KELEKIAN.
    Okay. Problem areas with Hex and Vin. *(He addresses all the Fellows, but Jason answers first and they resent him.)*
FELLOW 1.
    Myelosu —
JASON.   *(Interrupting.)*
    Well, first of course is myelosuppression, a lowering of blood-cell counts. It goes without saying. With this combination of agents, nephrotoxicity will be next.
KELEKIAN.
    Go on.
JASON.
    The kidneys are designed to filter out impurities in the blood-stream. In trying to filter the chemotherapeutic agent out of

the bloodstream, the kidneys shut down.

KELEKIAN.

Intervention.

JASON.

Hydration.

KELEKIAN.

Monitoring.

JASON.

Full recording of fluid intake and output, as you see here on these graphs, to monitor hydration and kidney function. Totals monitored daily by the clinical fellow, as per the protocol.

KELEKIAN.

Anybody else. Side effects.

FELLOW 1.

Nausea and vomiting.

KELEKIAN.

Jason.

JASON.

Routine.

FELLOW 2.

Pain while urinating.

JASON.

Routine. *(The Fellows are trying to catch Jason.)*

FELLOW 3.

Psychological depression.

JASON.

No way. *(The Fellows are silent.)*

KELEKIAN. *(Standing by Vivian the head of the bed.)*

Anything else. Other complaints with Hexamethophosphacil and Vinplatin. Come on. *(Silence. Kelekian and Vivian wait together for the correct answer.)*

FELLOW 4.

Mouth sores.

JASON.

Not yet.

FELLOW 2. *(Timidly.)*

Skin rash?

JASON.

Nope.

KELEKIAN. *(Sharing this with Vivian.)*

Why do we waste our time, Dr. Bearing?

VIVIAN. *(Delighted.)*

I do not know, Dr. Kelekian.

KELEKIAN. *(To the Fellows.)*

Use your eyes. *(All Fellows look closely at Vivian.)* Jesus God. Hair loss.

FELLOWS. *(All protesting. Vivian and Kelekian are amused.)*

— Come on.

— You can see it.

— It doesn't count.

— No fair.

KELEKIAN.

Jason.

JASON. *(Begrudgingly.)*

Hair loss after first cycle of treatment.

KELEKIAN.

That's better. *(To Vivian.)* Dr. Bearing. Full dose. Excellent. Keep pushing the fluids. *(The Fellows leave. Kelekian stops Jason.)* Jason.

JASON.

Huh?

KELEKIAN.

Clinical.

JASON.

Oh, right. *(To Vivian.)* Thank you, Professor Bearing. You've been very cooperative. *(They leave her with her stomach uncovered.)*

VIVIAN.

Wasn't that ... Grand? *(She gets up without the IV pole.)* At times, this obsessively detailed examination, this *scrutiny* seems to me to be a nefarious business. On the other hand, what is the alternative? Ignorance? Ignorance may be ... bliss; but it is not a very noble goal.

So I play my part. *(Pause.)*

I receive chemotherapy, throw up, am subjected to countless indignities, feel better, go home. Eight cycles. Eight neat little strophes. Oh, there have been the usual variations, subplots, red herrings: hepatotoxicity (liver poison), neuropathy (nerve death).

(Righteously.) They are medical terms. I look them up.

It has always been my custom to treat words with respect.

I can recall the time — the very hour of the very day — when I knew words would be my life's work.

(Scene change. A pile of six little white books appears, with Mr. Bearing, Vivian's father, seated behind an open newspaper.) It was my fifth birthday. *(Vivian, now a child, flops down to the books.)* I liked that one best.

MR. BEARING.   *(Disinterested but tolerant, never distracted from his newspaper.)*

Read another.

VIVIAN.

I think I'll read ... *(She takes a book from the stack and reads its spine intently.)* The Tale of the Flopsy Bunnies. *(Reading the front cover.)* The Tale of the Flopsy Bunnies. It has little bunnies on the front. *(Opening to the title page)*

The Tale of the Flopsy Bunnies by Beatrix Potter. *(She turns the page and begins to read.)*

It is said that the effect of eating too much lettuce is sopor
— sop — or —

what is that word?

MR. BEARING.

Sound it out.

VIVIAN.

Sop — or — fic. Sop — or — i — fic. Soporific. What does that mean?

MR. BEARING.

Soporific. Causing sleep.

VIVIAN.
Causing sleep.
MR. BEARING.
Makes you sleepy.
VIVIAN.
"Soporific" means "makes you sleepy"?
MR. BEARING.
Correct.
VIVIAN.
"Soporific" means "makes you sleepy." Soporific.
MR. BEARING.
Now use it in a sentence. What has a soporific effect on you?
VIVIAN.
A soporific effect on me.
MR. BEARING.
What makes you sleepy?
VIVIAN.
Aahh — nothing.
MR. BEARING.
Correct.
VIVIAN.
What about you?
MR. BEARING.
What has a soporific effect on me? Let me think: boring conversation, I suppose, after dinner.
VIVIAN.
Me too, boring conversation.
MR. BEARING.
Carry on.
VIVIAN.

It is said that the effect of eating too much lettuce is soporific.

The little bunnies in the picture are asleep! They're sleeping! Like you said, because of *soporific!* (*She stands up, and Mr. Bearing exits.*)

The illustration bore out the meaning of the word, just as he had explained it. At the time, it seemed like magic.

So imagine the effect that the words of John Donne first had on me: ratiocination, concatenation, coruscation, tergiversation.

Medical terms are less evocative. Still, I want to know what the doctors mean when they ... anatomize me. And I will grant that in this particular field of endeavor they possess a more potent arsenal of terminology than I. My only defense is the acquisition of vocabulary.

(Scene change. Susie enters and puts her arm around Vivian's shoulders to hold her up. Vivian is shaking, feverish, and weak. All at once.) Fever-and-neutropenia.

SUSIE.
When did it start?

VIVIAN.   *(Having difficulty speaking.)*
I — I was at home — reading — and I — felt so bad. I called. Fever and neutropenia. They said to come in.

SUSIE.
You did the right thing to come. Did somebody drive you?

VIVIAN.
Cab. I took a taxi.

SUSIE.   *(She grabs a wheelchair and helps Vivian sit. As Susie speaks, she takes Vivian's temperature, pulse, and respiration rate.)*
Here, why don't you sit? Just sit there a minute. I'll get Jason. He's on call tonight. We'll get him to give you some meds. I'm glad I was here on nights. I'll make sure you get to bed soon, okay? It'll just be a minute. I'll get you some juice, some nice juice with lots of ice. *(Susie leaves quickly. Vivian sits there, agitated, confused, and very sick. Susie returns with the juice.)*

VIVIAN.
Lights. I left all the lights on at my house.

SUSIE.
Don't you worry. It'll be all right. *(Jason enters, roused from his sleep and not fully awake. He wears surgical scrubs and puts on a lab coat as he enters.)*

JASON.   *(Without looking at Vivian.)*
How are you feeling, Professor Bearing?

37

VIVIAN.

My teeth — are chattering.

JASON.

Vitals.

SUSIE. *(Giving Vivian juice and a straw, without looking at Jason.)*

Temp 39.4. Pulse 120. Respiration 36. Chills and sweating.

JASON.

Fever and neutropenia. It's a "shake and bake." Blood cultures and urine, stat. Admit her. Prepare for reverse isolation. Start with acetaminophen. Vitals every four hours. *(He starts to leave.)*

SUSIE. *(Following him.)*

Jason — I think you need to talk to Kelekian about lowering the dose for the next cycle. It's too much for her like this.

JASON.

Lower the dose? No way. Full dose. She's tough. She can take it. Wake me up when the counts come from the lab. *(He pads off. Susie wheels Vivian to her room, and Vivian collapses on the bed. Susie connects Vivian's IV, then wets a washcloth and rubs her face and neck. Vivian remains delirious. Susie checks the IV and leaves with the wheelchair.)*

(After a while, Kelekian appears in the doorway holding a surgical mask near his face. Jason is with him, now dressed and clean-shaven.)

KELEKIAN.

Good morning, Dr. Bearing. Fifth cycle. Full dose. Definite progress. Everything okay.

VIVIAN. *(Weakly.)*

Yes.

KELEKIAN.

You're doing swell. Isolation is no problem. Couple of days. Think of it as a vacation.

VIVIAN.

Oh. *(Jason starts to enter, holding a mask near his face, just like Kelekian.)*

KELEKIAN.

Jason.

JASON.

Oh, Jesus. Okay, okay. *(He returns to the doorway, where he puts on a paper gown, mask, and gloves. Kelekian leaves.)*

VIVIAN. *(To audience.)*

In isolation, I am isolated. For once I can use a term literally. The chemotherapeutic agents eradicating my cancer have also eradicated my immune system. In my present condition, every living thing is a health hazard to me ... *(Jason comes in to check the intake-and-output.)*

JASON. *(Complaining to himself.)*

I really have not got time for this ...

VIVIAN.

... particularly health-care professionals.

JASON. *(Going right to the graph on the wall.)*

Just to look at the I&O sheets for one minute, and it takes me half an hour to do precautions. Four, seven, eleven. Two-fifty twice. Okay. *(Remembering.)* Oh, Jeez. Clinical. Professor Bearing. How are you feeling today?

VIVIAN. *(Very sick.)*

Fine. Just shaking sometimes from the chills.

JASON.

IV will kick in anytime now. No problem. Listen, gotta go. Keep pushing the fluids. *(As he exits, he takes off the gown, mask, and gloves.)*

VIVIAN. *(Getting up from bed with her IV pole and resuming her explanation.)*

I am not in isolation because I have cancer, because I have a tumor the size of a grapefruit. No. I am in isolation because I am being treated for cancer. My treatment imperils my health.

Herein lies the paradox. John Donne would revel in it. I would revel in it, if he wrote a poem about it. My students would flounder in it, because paradox is too difficult to understand. Think of it as a puzzle, I would tell them, an intellectual game. *(She is trapped.)*

Or, I *would have* told them. Were it a game. Which it is not.

(Escaping.) If they were here, if I were lecturing: How I would *perplex* them! I could work my students into a frenzy.

Every ambiguity, every shifting awareness. I could draw so much from the poems.

I could be so powerful.

(Scene change. Vivian stands still, as if conjuring a scene. Now at the height of her powers, she grandly disconnects herself from the IV. Technicians remove the bed and hand her a pointer.) The poetry of the early seventeenth century, what has been called the metaphysical school, considers an intractable mental puzzle by exercising the outstanding human faculty of the era, namely wit.

The greatest wit — the greatest English poet, some would say — was John Donne. In the Holy Sonnets, Donne applied his capacious, agile wit to the larger aspects of the human experience: life, death, and God.

In his poems, metaphysical quandaries are addressed, but never resolved. Ingenuity, virtuosity, and a vigorous intellect that jousts with the most exalted concepts: these are the tools of wit. *(The lights dim. A screen lowers, and the sonnet "If poysonous mineralls," from the Gardner edition, appears on it. Vivian recites.)*

> If poysonous mineralls, and if that tree,
> Whose fruit threw death on else immortall us,
> If lecherous goats, if serpents envious
> Cannot be damn'd; Alas; why should I bee?
> Why should intent or reason, borne in mee,
> Make sinnes, else equall, in mee, more heinous?
> And mercy being easie, 'and glorious
> To God, in his sterne wrath, why threatens hee?
> But who am I, that dare dispute with thee?
> O God, Oh! of thine onely worthy blood,
> And my teares, make a heavenly Lethean flood,
> And drowne in it my sinnes blacke memorie.
> That thou remember them, some claime as debt,
> I thinke it mercy, if thou wilt forget.

(Vivian whacks the word on the screen with a pointer at every asterisk (*). She moves around as she lectures.)

Aggressive intellect. *(*Line 1.)* Pious melodrama. *(*Line 10.)* And a final, fearful point. *(*Line 14.)* Donne's Holy

Sonnet Five, 1609. From the Ashford edition, based on Gardner.

The speaker of the sonnet has a brilliant mind, and he plays the part convincingly; but in the end he finds God's *forgiveness* hard to believe, so he crawls under a rock to *hide.*

If*(*)* arsenic *(*mineralls)* and serpents*(*)* are not damned, then why is he? In asking the question, the speaker turns eternal damnation into an intellectual game. Why would God choose to do what is *hard,* to condemn, rather than what is *easy,* and also *glorious* — to show mercy?

(Several scholars have disputed Ashford's third comma*(*)* in line six, but none convincingly.)

But.*(*)* Exception. Limitation. Contrast. The argument shifts from cleverness to melodrama, an unconvincing eruption of piety: "O"*(*)* "God"*(*)* "Oh."*(*)*

A typical prayer would plead "Remember me, O Lord." (This point is nicely explicated in an article by Richard Strier — a former student of mine who once sat where you do now, although I dare say *he* was *awake* — in the May 1989 issue of *Modern Philology.*) True believers ask to be *remembered* by God. The speaker of this sonnet asks God to *forget.(*)* *(Vivian moves in front of the screen, and the projection of the poem is cast directly upon her.)* Where is the hyperactive intellect of the first section? Where is the histrionic outpouring of the second? When the speaker considers his own *sins,* and the inevitability of God's *judgment,* he can conceive of but one resolution: to *disappear. (Vivian moves away from the screen.)* Doctrine assures us that no sinner is denied *forgiveness,* not even one whose sins are overweening *intellect (*Top half.)* or overwrought *dramatics. (*Bottom half.)* The speaker does not need to *hide* from God's *judgment,* only to *accept* God's *forgiveness.* It is very simple. Suspiciously simple.

We want to correct the speaker, to remind him of the assurance of salvation. But it is too late. The poetic encounter is over. We are left to our own consciences. Have we outwitted Donne? Or have we been outwitted? *(Susie comes on.)*
SUSIE.
Ms. Bearing?

VIVIAN. *(Continuing.)*
Will the po —
SUSIE.
Ms. Bearing?
VIVIAN. *(Crossly.)*
What is it?
SUSIE.
You have to go down for a test. Jason just called. They want
another ultrasound. They're concerned about a bowel
obstruction — Is it okay if I come in?
VIVIAN.
No. Not now.
SUSIE.
I'm sorry, but they want it now.
VIVIAN.
Not right now. It's not *supposed* to be now.
SUSIE.
Yes, they want to do it now. I've got the chair.
VIVIAN.
It should not be now. I am in the middle of — this. I have *this*
planned for now, not ultrasound. No more tests. We've cov-
ered that.
SUSIE.
I know, I know, but they need for it to be now. It won't take
long, and it isn't a bad procedure. Why don't you just come
along.
VIVIAN.
I do not want to go now!
SUSIE.
Ms. Bearing. *(Silence. Vivian raises the screen, walks away from the
scene, hooks herself to the IV, and gets in the wheelchair. Susie wheels
Vivian, and a Technician takes her.)*
TECHNICIAN.
Name.
VIVIAN.
B-E-A-R-I-N-G. Kelekian.
TECHNICIAN.
It'll just be a minute.

42

VIVIAN.
Time for your break.
TECHNICIAN.
Yup. *(The Technician leaves.)*
VIVIAN.   *(Mordantly.)*
Take a break! *(Scene change. Vivian sits weakly in the wheelchair.)*

> This is my playes last scene, here heavens appoint
> My pilgrimages last mile; and my race
> Idly, yet quickly runne, hath this last pace,
> My spans last inch, my minutes last point,
> And gluttonous death will instantly unjoynt
> My body, 'and soule

John Donne. 1609. I have always particularly liked that poem. In the abstract. Now I find the image of "my minute's last point" a little too, shall we say, *pointed*.

I don't mean to complain, but I am becoming very sick. Very, very sick. Ultimately sick, as it were.

In everything I have done, I have been steadfast, resolute — some would say in the extreme. Now, as you can see, I am distinguishing myself in illness.

I have survived eight treatments of Hexamethophosphacil and Vinplatin at the *full* dose, ladies and gentlemen. I have broken the record. I have become something of a celebrity. Kelekian and Jason are simply delighted. I think they foresee celebrity status for themselves upon the appearance of the journal article they will no doubt write about me.

But I flatter myself. The article will not be about me, it will be about my ovaries. It will be about my peritoneal cavity, which, despite their best intentions, is now crawling with cancer.

What we have come to think of as *me* is, in fact, just the specimen jar, just the dust jacket, just the white piece of paper that bears the little black marks.

My next line is supposed to be something like this:

"It is such a *relief* to get back to my room after those infernal tests."

This is hardly true. It would be a *relief* to be a cheerleader on her way to Daytona Beach for Spring Break.

To get back to my room after those infernal tests is just the next thing that happens.

(Scene change. She returns to her bed, which now has a commode next to it. She is very sick.) Oh, God. It is such a relief to get back to my goddamn room after those goddamn tests. *(Jason enters.)*

JASON.

Professor Bearing. Just want to check the I&O. Four-fifty, six, five. Okay. How are you feeling today? *(He makes notations on his clipboard throughout the scene.)*

VIVIAN.

Fine.

JASON.

That's great. Just great.

VIVIAN.

How are my fluids?

JASON.

Pretty good. No kidney involvement yet. That's pretty amazing, with Hex and Vin.

VIVIAN.

How will you know when the kidneys are involved?

JASON.

Lots of in, not much out.

VIVIAN.

That simple.

JASON.

Oh, no way. Compromised kidney function is a highly complex reaction. I'm simplifying for you.

VIVIAN.

Thank you.

JASON.

We're supposed to.

VIVIAN.

Bedside manner.

JASON.

Yeah, there's a whole course on it in med school. It's

44

required. Colossal waste of time for researchers. *(He turns to go.)*

VIVIAN.

I can imagine. *(Trying to ask something important.)* Jason?

JASON.

Huh?

VIVIAN.   *(Not sure of herself.)*

Ah, what ... *(Quickly.)* What were you just saying?

JASON.

When?

VIVIAN.

Never mind.

JASON.

Professor Bearing?

VIVIAN.

Yes.

JASON.

Are you experiencing confusion? Short-term memory loss?

VIVIAN.

No.

JASON.

Sure?

VIVIAN.

Yes. *(Pause.)* I was just wondering: why cancer?

JASON.

Why cancer?

VIVIAN.

Why not open-heart surgery?

JASON.

Oh yeah, why not *plumbing*. Why not run a *lube rack*, for all the surgeons know about *Homo sapiens sapiens*. No way. Cancer's the only thing I ever wanted.

VIVIAN.   *(Intrigued.)*

Huh.

JASON.

No, really. Cancer is ... *(Searching.)*

VIVIAN.   *(Helping.)*

Awesome.

JASON. *(Pause.)*

Yeah. Yeah, that's right. It is. It is awesome. How does it do it? The intercellular regulatory mechanisms — especially for proliferation and differentiation — the malignant neoplasia just don't get it. You grow normal cells in tissue culture in the lab, and they replicate just enough to make a nice, confluent monolayer. They divide twenty times, or fifty times, but eventually they conk out. You grow cancer cells, and they never stop. No contact inhibition whatsoever. They just pile up, just keep replicating forever. *(Pause.)* That's got a funny name. Know what it is?

VIVIAN.

No. What?

JASON.

Immortality in culture.

VIVIAN.

Sounds like a symposium.

JASON.

It's an error in judgment, in a molecular way. But *why?* Even on the protistic level the normal cell-cell interactions are so subtle they'll take your breath away. Golden-brown algae, for instance, the lowest multicellular life form on earth — they're *idiots* — and it's incredible. It's perfect. So what's up with the cancer cells? Smartest guys in the world, with the best labs, funding — they don't know what to make of it.

VIVIAN.

What about you?

JASON.

Me? Oh, I've got a couple of ideas, things I'm kicking around. Wait till I get a lab of my own. If I can survive this ... *fellowship.*

VIVIAN.

The part with the human beings.

JASON.

Everybody's got to go through it. All the great researchers. They want us to be able to converse intelligently with the clinicians. As though *researchers* were the impediments. The clinicians are such troglodytes. So smarmy. Like we have to hold

46

hands to discuss creatinine clearance. Just cut the crap, I say.

VIVIAN.

Are you going to be sorry when — Do you ever miss people?

JASON.

Everybody asks that. Especially girls.

VIVIAN.

What do you tell them?

JASON.

I tell them yes.

VIVIAN.

Are they persuaded?

JASON.

Some.

VIVIAN.

Some. I see. *(With great difficulty.)* And what do you say when a patient is ... apprehensive ... frightened.

JASON.

Of who?

VIVIAN.

I just ... Never mind.

JASON.

Professor Bearing, who is the President of the United States?

VIVIAN.

I'm fine, really. It's all right.

JASON.

You sure? I could order a test —

VIVIAN.

No! No, I'm fine. Just a little tired.

JASON.

Okay. Look. Gotta go. Keep pushing the fluids. Try for 2,000 a day, okay?

VIVIAN.

Okay. To use your word. Okay. *(Jason leaves. Getting out of bed, without her IV.)*

So. The young doctor, like the senior scholar, prefers research to humanity. At the same time the senior scholar, in her pathetic state as a simpering victim, wishes the young

47

doctor would take more interest in personal contact.

Now I suppose we shall see, through a series of flash-backs, how the senior scholar ruthlessly denied her simpering students the touch of human kindness she now seeks.

(Scene change. Students appear, sitting at chairs with writing desks attached to the right arm. She suddenly commands attention.) How then would you characterize *(Pointing to a student.)* — you.

STUDENT 1.

Huh?

VIVIAN.

How would you characterize the animating force of this sonnet?

STUDENT 1.

Huh?

VIVIAN.

In this sonnet, what is the principal poetic device? I'll give you a hint. It has nothing to do with football. What propels this sonnet?

STUDENT 1.

Um.

VIVIAN. *(Speaking to the audience.)*

Did I say *(Tenderly.)* "You are nineteen years old. You are so young. You don't know a sonnet from a steak sandwich." *(Pause.)* By no means.

(Sharply, to Student 1.) You can come to this class prepared, or you can excuse yourself from this class, this department, and this university. Do not think for a moment that I will tolerate anything in between.

(To the audience, defensively.) I was teaching him a lesson. *(She walks away from Student 1, then turns and addresses the class.)*

So we have another instance of John Donne's agile wit at work: not so much *resolving* the issues of life and God as *reveling* in their complexity.

STUDENT 2.

But why?

VIVIAN.

Why what?

48

STUDENT 2.

Why does Donne make everything so *complicated? (The other students laugh in agreement.)* No, really, *why?*

VIVIAN.   *(To the audience.)*

You know, someone asked me that every year. And it was always one of the smart ones. What could I say? *(To Student 2.)* What do you think?

STUDENT 2.

I think it's like he's hiding. I think he's really confused, I don't know, maybe he's scared, so he hides behind all this complicated stuff, hides behind this *wit.*

VIVIAN.

Hides behind *wit?*

STUDENT 2.

I mean, if it's really something he's sure of, he can say it more simple — simply. He doesn't have to be such a brain, or such a performer. It doesn't have to be such a big deal. *(The other students encourage him.)*

VIVIAN.

Perhaps he is suspicious of simplicity.

STUDENT 2.

Perhaps, but that's pretty stupid.

VIVIAN.   *(To the audience.)*

That observation, despite its infelicitous phrasing, contained the seed of a perspicacious remark. Such an unlikely occurrence left me with two choices. I could draw it out, or I could allow the brain to rest after that heroic effort. If I pursued, there was the chance of great insight, or the risk of undergraduate banality. I could never predict. *(To Student 2.)* Go on.

STUDENT 2.

Well, if he's trying to figure out God, and the meaning of life, and big stuff like that, why does he keep running away, you know?

VIVIAN.   *(To the audience, moving closer to student 2.)*

So far so good, but they can think for themselves only so long before they begin to self-destruct.

STUDENT 2.

Um, it's like, the more you hide, the less — no, wait — the

more you are getting closer — although you don't know it — and the simple thing is there — you see what I mean?

VIVIAN. *(To the audience, looking at Student 2, as suspense collapses.)*

Lost it.

(She walks away and speaks to the audience.) I distinctly remember an exchange between two students after my lecture on pronunciation and scansion. I overheard them talking on their way out of class. They were young and bright, gathering their books and laughing at the expense of seventeenth-century poetry, at my expense.

(To the class.) To scan the line properly, we must take advantage of the contemporary flexibility in "i-o-n" endings, as in "expansion." The quatrain stands:

Our two souls therefore, which are one,
    Though I must go, endure not yet
A breach, but an ex-*pan*-see-on,
    Like gold to airy thinness beat.

Bear this in mind in your reading. That's all for today. *(The Students get up in a chaotic burst. Student 3 and Student 4 pass by Vivian on their way out.)*

STUDENT 3.

I hope I can get used to this pronuncia-see-on.

STUDENT 4.

I know. I hope I can survive this course and make it to gradua-see-on. *(They laugh. Vivian glowers at them. They fall silent, embarrassed.)*

VIVIAN. *(To the audience.)*

That was a witty little exchange, I must admit. It showed the mental acuity I would praise in a poetic text. But I admired only the studied application of wit, not its spontaneous eruption. *(Student 1 interrupts.)*

STUDENT 1.

Professor Bearing? Can I talk to you for a minute?

VIVIAN.

You may.

STUDENT 1.

I need to ask for an extension on my paper. I'm really sorry, and I know your policy, but see —

VIVIAN.

Don't tell me. Your grandmother died.

STUDENT 1.

You knew.

VIVIAN.

It was a guess.

STUDENT 1.

I have to go home.

VIVIAN.

Do what you will, but the paper is due when it is due. *(As Student 1 leaves and the classroom disappears, Vivian watches. Pause.)*

I don't know. I feel so much — what is the word? I look back, I see these scenes, and I ... *(Long silence. Vivian walks absently around the stage, trying to think of something. Finally, giving up, she trudges back to bed. Scene change.)*

It was late at night, the graveyard shift. Susie was on. I could hear her in the hall.

I wanted her to come and see me. So I had to create a little emergency. Nothing dramatic. *(Vivian pinches the IV tubing. The pump alarm beeps.)*

It worked. *(Susie enters, concerned.)*

SUSIE.

Ms. Bearing? Is that you beeping at four in the morning? *(She checks the tubing and presses buttons on the pump. The alarm stops.)* Did that wake you up? I'm sorry. It just gets occluded some-times.

VIVIAN.

I was awake.

SUSIE.

You were? What's the trouble, sweetheart?

VIVIAN. *(To the audience, roused.)*

Do not think for a minute that anyone calls me "Sweetheart." But then ... I allowed it. *(To Susie.)* Oh, I don't know.

SUSIE.

You can't sleep?

VIVIAN.

No. I just keep thinking.

SUSIE.

If you do that too much, you can get kind of confused.

VIVIAN.

I know. I can't figure things out. I'm in a ... *quandary,* having these ... *doubts.*

SUSIE.

What you're doing is very hard.

VIVIAN.

Hard things are what I like best.

SUSIE.

It's not the same. It's like it's out of control, isn't it?

VIVIAN.   *(Crying, in spite of herself.)*

I'm scared.

SUSIE.   *(Stroking her.)*

Oh, honey, of course you are.

VIVIAN.

I want ...

SUSIE.

I know. It's hard.

VIVIAN.

I don't feel sure of myself anymore.

SUSIE.

And you used to feel sure.

VIVIAN.   *(Crying.)*

Oh, yes, I used to feel sure.

SUSIE.

Vivian. It's all right. I know. It hurts. I know. It's all right. Do you want a tissue? It's all right. *(Silence.)* Vivian, would you like a Popsicle?

VIVIAN.   *(Like a child.)*

Yes, please.

SUSIE.

I'll get it for you. I'll be right back.

VIVIAN.

Thank you. *(Susie leaves. Pulling herself together.)* The epithelial cells in my GI tract have been killed by the chemo. The cold

Popsicle feels good, it's something I can digest, and it helps keep me hydrated. For your information.

(Susie returns with an orange two-stick Popsicle. Vivian unwraps it and breaks it in half.) Here.

SUSIE.

Sure?

VIVIAN.

Yes.

SUSIE.

Thanks. *(Susie sits on the commode by the bed. Silence.)* When I was a kid, we used to get these from a truck. The man would come around and ring his bell and we'd all run over. Then we'd sit on the curb and eat our Popsicles.

Pretty profound, huh?

VIVIAN.

It sounds nice. *(Silence.)*

SUSIE.

Vivian, there's something we need to talk about, you need to think about. *(Silence.)*

VIVIAN.

My cancer is not being cured, is it.

SUSIE.

Huh-uh.

VIVIAN.

They never expected it to be, did they.

SUSIE.

Well, they thought the drugs would make the tumor get smaller, and it has gotten a lot smaller. But the problem is that it started in new places too. They've learned a lot for their research. It was the best thing they had to give you, the strongest drugs. There just isn't a good treatment for what you have yet, for advanced ovarian. I'm sorry. They should have explained this —

VIVIAN.

I knew.

SUSIE.

You did.

VIVIAN.

I read between the lines.

SUSIE.

What you have to think about is your "code status." What you want them to do if your heart stops.

VIVIAN.

Well.

SUSIE.

You can be "full code," which means that if your heart stops, they'll call a Code Blue and the code team will come and resuscitate you and take you to Intensive Care until you stabilize again. Or you can be "Do Not Resuscitate," so if your heart stops we'll ... well, we'll just let it. You'll be "DNR." You can think about it, but I wanted to present both choices before Kelekian and Jason talk to you.

VIVIAN.

You don't agree about this?

SUSIE.

Well, they like to save lives. So anything's okay, as long as life continues. It doesn't matter if you're hooked up to a million machines. Kelekian is a great researcher and everything. And the fellows, like Jason, they're really smart. It's really an honor for them to work with him. But they always ... want to know more things.

VIVIAN.

I always want to know more things. I'm a scholar. Or I was when I had shoes, when I had eyebrows.

SUSIE.

Well, okay then. You'll be full code. That's fine. *(Silence.)*

VIVIAN.

No, don't complicate the matter.

SUSIE.

It's okay. It's up to you —

VIVIAN.

Let it stop.

SUSIE.

Really?

VIVIAN.

Yes.

SUSIE.

So if your heart stops beating —

VIVIAN.

Just let it stop.

SUSIE.

Sure?

VIVIAN.

Yes.

SUSIE.

Okay. I'll get Kelekian to give the order, and then —

VIVIAN.

Susie?

SUSIE.

Uh-huh?

VIVIAN.

You're still going to take care of me, aren't you?

SUSIE.

'Course, sweetheart. Don't you worry. *(As Susie leaves, Vivian sits upright, full of energy and rage.)*

VIVIAN.

That certainly was a *maudlin* display. Popsicles? "Sweetheart"? I can't believe my life has become so ... corny.

But it can't be helped. I don't see any other way. We are discussing life and death, and not in the abstract, either; we are discussing *my* life and *my* death, and my brain is dulling, and poor Susie's was never very sharp to begin with, and I can't conceive of any other ... *tone.*

(Quickly.) Now is not the time for verbal swordplay, for unlikely flights of imagination and wildly shifting perspectives, for metaphysical conceit, for wit.

And nothing would be worse than a detailed scholarly analysis. Erudition. Interpretation. Complication.

(Slowly.) Now is a time for simplicity. Now is a time for, dare I say it, kindness.

(Searchingly.) I thought being extremely smart would take

care of it. But I see that I have been found out. Ooohhh.

I'm scared. Oh, God. I want ... I want ... No. I want to hide. I just want to curl up in a little ball. *(She dives under the covers. Scene change. Vivian wakes in horrible pain. She is tense, agitated, fearful. Slowly she calms down and addresses the audience. Trying extremely hard.)*

I want to tell you how it feels. I want to explain it, to use *my* words. It's as if ... I can't ... There aren't ... I'm like a student and this is the final exam and I don't know what to put down because I don't understand the question and I'm *running out of time. (Pause.)*

The time for extreme measures has come. I am in terrible pain. Susie says that I need to begin aggressive pain management if I am going to stand it.

"It": such a little word. In this case, I think "it" signifies "being alive."

I apologize in advance for what this palliative treatment modality does to the dramatic coherence of my play's last scene. It can't be helped. They have to do something. I'm in terrible pain.

Say it, Vivian. *It hurts like hell. It really does. (Susie enters. Vivian is writhing in pain.)*

Oh, God. Oh, God.

SUSIE.
Sshh. It's okay. Sshh. I paged Kelekian up here, and we'll get you some meds.

VIVIAN.
Oh, God, it is so painful. So painful. So much pain. So much pain.

SUSIE.
I know, I know, it's okay. Sshh. Just try and clear your mind. It's all right. We'll get you a Patient-Controlled Analgesic. It's a little pump, and you push a little button, and you decide how much medication you want. *(Importantly.)* It's very simple, and it's up to you. *(Kelekian storms in; Jason follows with chart.)*

KELEKIAN.
Dr. Bearing. Susie.

SUSIE.

Time for Patient-Controlled Analgesic. The pain is killing her.

KELEKIAN.

Dr. Bearing, are you in pain? *(Kelekian holds out his hand for chart; Jason hands it to him. They read.)*

VIVIAN. *(Sitting up, unnoticed by the staff.)*

Am I in pain? I don't believe this. Yes, I'm in goddamn pain. *(Furious.)* I have a fever of 101 spiking to 104. And I have bone metastases in my pelvis and both femurs. *(Screaming.)* There is cancer eating away at my goddamn bones, and I did not know there could be such pain on this earth.

(She flops back on the bed and cries audibly to them.) Oh, God.

KELEKIAN. *(Looking at Vivian intently.)*

I want a morphine drip.

SUSIE.

What about Patient-Controlled? She could be more alert —

KELEKIAN. *(Teaching.)*

Ordinarily, yes. But in her case, no.

SUSIE.

But —

KELEKIAN. *(To Susie.)*

She's earned a rest. *(To Jason.)* Morphine, ten push now, then start at ten an hour. *(To Vivian.)* Dr. Bearing, try to relax. We're going to help you through this, don't worry. Dr. Bearing? Excellent. *(He squeezes Vivian's shoulder. They all leave.)*

VIVIAN. *(Weakly, painfully, leaning on her IV pole, she moves to address the audience.)*

Hi. How are you feeling today? *(Silence.)*

These are my last coherent lines. I'll have to leave the action to the professionals.

It came so quickly, after taking so long. Not even time for a proper conclusion. *(Vivian concentrates with all her might, and she attempts a grand summation, as if trying to conjure her own ending.)*

And Death — *capital D* — shall be no more — *semicolon.* Death — *capital D* — thou shalt die — *ex-cla-mation point!*

(She looks down at herself, looks out at the audience, and sees that the line doesn't work. She shakes her head and exhales with resignation.) I'm sorry.

 (Scene change. She gets back into bed as Susie injects morphine into the IV tubing. Vivian lies down and, in a final melodramatic gesture, shuts the lids of her own eyes and folds her arms over her chest.) I trust this will have a soporific effect.

SUSIE.

Well, I don't know about that, but it sure makes you sleepy. *(This strikes Vivian as delightfully funny. She starts to giggle, then laughs out loud. Susie doesn't get it.)* What's so funny? *(Vivian keeps laughing.)* What?

VIVIAN.

Oh! It's that — "Soporific" *means* "makes you sleepy."

SUSIE.

It does?

VIVIAN.

Yes. *(Another fit of laughter.)*

SUSIE. *(Giggling.)*

Well, that was pretty dumb —

VIVIAN.

No! No, no! It was *funny!*

SUSIE. *(Starting to catch on.)*

Yeah, I guess so. *(Laughing.)* In a dumb sort of way. *(This sets them both off laughing again.)* I never would have gotten it. I'm glad you explained it.

VIVIAN. *(Simply.)*

I'm a teacher. *(They laugh a little together. Slowly the morphine kicks in, and Vivian's laughs become long sighs. Finally she falls asleep. Susie checks everything out, then leaves. Long silence. Scene change. Jason and Susie chat as they enter to insert a catheter.)*

JASON.

Oh, yeah. She was a great scholar. Wrote tons of books, articles, was the head of everything. *(He checks the I&O sheet.)* Two hundred. Seventy-five. Five-twenty. Let's up the hydration. She won't be drinking anymore. See if we can keep her kidneys from fading. Yeah, I had a lot of respect for her, which is more than I can say for the *entire* biochemistry department.

SUSIE.

What do you want? Dextrose?

JASON.

Give her saline.

SUSIE.

Okay.

JASON.

She gave a hell of a lecture. No notes, not a word out of place. It was pretty impressive. A lot of students hated her, though.

SUSIE.

Why?

JASON.

Well, she wasn't exactly a cupcake.

SUSIE. *(Laughing, fondly.)*

Well, she hasn't exactly been a cupcake here, either. *(Leaning over Vivian and talking loudly and slowly in her ear.)* Now, Ms. Bearing, Jason and I are here, and we're going to insert a catheter to collect your urine. It's not going to hurt, don't you worry. *(During the conversation she inserts the catheter.)*

JASON.

Like she can hear you.

SUSIE.

It's just nice to do.

JASON.

Eight cycles of Hex and Vin at the full dose. Kelekian didn't think it was possible. I wish they could all get through it at full throttle. Then we could really have some data.

SUSIE.

She's not what I imagined. I thought somebody who studied poetry would be sort of dreamy, you know?

JASON.

Oh, not the way she did it. It felt more like boot camp than English class. This guy John Donne was incredibly intense. Like your whole brain had to be in knots before you could get it.

SUSIE.

He made it hard on purpose?

JASON.

Well, it has to do with the subject. The Holy Sonnets we worked on most, they were mostly about Salvation Anxiety. That's a term I made up in one of my papers, but I think it fits pretty well. Salvation Anxiety. You're this brilliant guy, I mean, brilliant — this guy makes Shakespeare sound like a Hallmark card. And you know you're a sinner. And there's this promise of salvation, the whole religious thing. But you just can't deal with it.

SUSIE.

How come?

JASON.

It just doesn't stand up to scrutiny. But you can't face life without it either. So you write these screwed-up sonnets. Everything is brilliantly convoluted. Really tricky stuff. Bouncing off the walls. Like a game, to make the puzzle so complicated. *(The catheter is inserted. Susie puts things away.)*

SUSIE.

But what happens in the end?

JASON.

End of what?

SUSIE.

To John Donne. Does he ever get it?

JASON.

Get what?

SUSIE.

His Salvation Anxiety. Does he ever understand?

JASON.

Oh, no way. The puzzle takes over. You're not even trying to solve it anymore. Fascinating, really. Great training for lab research. Looking at things in increasing levels of complexity.

SUSIE.

Until what?

JASON.

What do you mean?

SUSIE.

Where does it end? Don't you get to solve the puzzle?

JASON.

Nah. When it comes right down to it, research is just trying to quantify the complications of the puzzle.

SUSIE.

But you *help* people! You save lives and stuff.

JASON.

Oh, yeah, I save some guy's life, and then the poor slob gets hit by a bus!

SUSIE. *(Confused.)*

Yeah, I guess so. I just don't think of it that way. Guess you can tell I never took a class in poetry.

JASON.

Listen, if there's one thing we learned in Seventeenth-Century Poetry, it's that you can forget about that sentimental stuff. *Enzyme Kinetics* was more poetic than Bearing's class. Besides, you can't think about that *meaning-of-life* garbage all the time or you'd go nuts.

SUSIE.

Do you believe in it?

JASON.

In what?

SUSIE.

Umm. I don't know, the meaning-of-life garbage. *(She laughs a little.)*

JASON.

What do they *teach* you in nursing school? *(Checking Vivian's pulse.)* She's out of it. Shouldn't be too long. You done here?

SUSIE.

Yeah, I'll just ... tidy up.

JASON.

See ya. *(He leaves.)*

SUSIE.

Bye, Jace. *(She thinks for a minute, then carefully rubs baby oil on Vivian's hands. She checks the catheter, then leaves. Scene change. Professor E. M. Ashford, now eighty, enters.)*

E.M.

Vivian? Vivian? It's Evelyn. Vivian?

VIVIAN. *(Waking, slurred.)*

Oh, God. *(Surprised.)* Professor Ashford. Oh, God.

61

E.M.

I'm in town visiting my great-grandson, who is celebrating his fifth birthday. I went to see you at your office, and they directed me here. *(She lays her jacket, scarf, and parcel on the bed.)* I have been walking all over town. I had forgotten how early it gets chilly here.

VIVIAN. *(Weakly.)*

I feel so bad.

E.M.

I know you do. I can see. *(Vivian cries.)* Oh, dear, there, there. There, there. *(Vivian cries more, letting the tears flow.)* Vivian, Vivian.

(E.M. looks toward the hall, then furtively slips off her shoes and swings up on the bed. She puts her arm around Vivian.) There, there. There, there, Vivian. *(Silence.)*

It's a windy day. *(Silence.)*

Don't worry, dear. *(Silence.)*

Let's see. Shall I recite to you? Would you like that? I'll recite something by Donne.

VIVIAN. *(Moaning.)*

Nooooooo.

E.M.

Very well. *(Silence.)* Hmmm. *(Silence.)* Little Jeffrey is very sweet. Gets into everything.

(Silence. E.M. takes a children's book out of the paper bag and begins reading. Vivian nestles in, drifting in and out of sleep.) Let's see. *The Runaway Bunny.* By Margaret Wise Brown. Pictures by Clement Hurd. Copyright 1942. First Harper Trophy Edition, 1972.

Now then.

Once there was a little bunny who wanted to run away.
So he said to his mother, "I am running away."

"If you run away," said his mother, "I will run after you.
For you are my little bunny."

"If you run after me," said the little bunny, "I will become
a fish in a trout stream and I will swim away from you."

"If you become a fish in a trout stream," said his mother, "I will become a fisherman and I will fish for you."

(Thinking out loud.) Look at that. A little allegory of the soul. No matter where it hides, God will find it. See, Vivian?
VIVIAN. *(Moaning.)*
Uhhhhhh.
E.M.

"If you become a fisherman," said the little bunny, "I will be a bird and fly away from you."

"If you become a bird and fly away from me," said his mother, "I will be a tree that you come home to."

(To herself.) Very clever.

"Shucks," said the little bunny, "I might just as well stay where I am and be your little bunny."
And so he did.

"Have a carrot," said the mother bunny.
(To herself.) Wonderful. *(Vivian is now fast asleep. E.M. slowly gets down and gathers her things. She leans over and kisses her.)*

It's time to go. And flights of angels sing thee to thy rest.

(She leaves. Jason strides in and goes directly to the I&O sheet without looking at Vivian.)
JASON.
Professor Bearing. How are you feeling today? Three P.M. IV hydration totals. Two thousand in. Thirty out. Uh-oh. That's it. Kidneys gone.
(He looks at Vivian.) Professor Bearing? Highly unresponsive. Wait a second — *(Puts his head down to her mouth and chest to listen for heartbeat and breathing.)* Wait a sec — Jesus Christ! *(Yelling.)* CALL A CODE! *(Jason throws down the chart, dives over the bed, and lies on top of her body as he reaches for the phone and punches in the numbers. To himself.)*

Code: 4-5-7-5. *(To operator.)* Code Blue, room 707. Code Blue, room 707. Dr. Posner — P-O-S-N-E-R. Hurry up!

(He throws down the phone and lowers the head of the bed.) Come on, come on, COME ON.

(He begins CPR, kneeling over Vivian, alternately pounding frantically and giving mouth-to-mouth resuscitation. Over the loudspeaker in the hall, a droning voice repeats "Code Blue, room 707. Code Blue, room 707.") One! Two! Three! Four! Five! *(He breathes in her mouth. Susie, hearing the announcement, runs into the room.)*

SUSIE.
WHAT ARE YOU DOING?

JASON.
A GODDAMN CODE. GET OVER HERE!

SUSIE.
She's DNR! *(She grabs him.)*

JASON. *(He pushes Susie away.)*
She's Research!

SUSIE.
She's NO CODE! *(She grabs Jason and hurls him off the bed.)*

JASON.
Ooowww! Goddamnit, Susie!

SUSIE.
She's no code!

JASON.
Aaargh!

SUSIE.
Kelekian put the order in — you saw it! You were right there, Jason! Oh, God, the code! *(She runs to the phone. Jason struggles to stand. Into the phone.)* 4-5-7-5.

(The code team swoops in. Everything changes. Frenzy takes over. The code team knock Susie out of the way with their equipment. Susie, into the phone.) Cancel code, room 707. Sue Monahan, primary nurse. Cancel code. Dr. Posner is here.

JASON. *(In agony.)*
Oh, God.

CODE TEAM.
— Get out of the way!

— Unit staff out!

— Get the board!

— Over here! *(They throw Vivian's body up at the waist and stick a board underneath for CPR. In a whirlwind of sterile packaging and barked commands, one team member attaches a respirator, one begins CPR, and one prepares the defibrillator. Susie and Jason try to stop them but are pushed away. The loudspeaker in the hall announces "Cancel code, room 707. Cancel code, room 707.")*

— Bicarb amp!

— I got it! *(To Susie.)* Get out!

— One, two, three, four, five!

— Get ready to shock! *(To Jason.)* Move it!

SUSIE. *(Running to each person, yelling.)*

STOP! Patient is DNR!

JASON. *(At the same time, to the code team.)*

No, no! Stop doing this. STOP!

CODE TEAM.

— Keep it going!

— What do you get?

— Bicarb amp!

— No pulse!

SUSIE.

She's NO CODE! Order was given — *(She dives for the chart and holds it up as she cries out.)* Look! Look at this! DO NOT RESUSCITATE. KELEKIAN.

CODE TEAM. *(As they administer electric shock, Vivian's body arches and bounces back down.)*

— Almost ready!

— Hit her!

— CLEAR!

— Pulse? Pulse?

JASON. *(Howling.)*

I MADE A MISTAKE! *(Pause. The code team looks at him. He collapses on the floor.)*

SUSIE.

No code! Patient is no code.

CODE TEAM HEAD.

Who the hell are you?

SUSIE.
Sue Monahan, primary nurse.
CODE TEAM HEAD.
Let me see the goddamn chart. CHART!
CODE TEAM.   *(Slowing down.)*
    — What's going on?
    — Should we stop?
    — What's it say?
SUSIE.   *(Pushing them away from the bed.)*
Patient is no code. Get away from her!

(Susie lifts the blanket.
Vivian steps out of the bed.

She walks away from the
scene, toward a little light.

She is now attentive and
eager, moving slowly toward
the light.

She takes off her cap and lets
it drop.

She slips off her bracelet.

She loosens the ties and the
top gown slides to the floor.
She lets the second gown
fall.

The instant she is naked,
and beautiful, reaching for
the light —

Lights out.)

CODE TEAM HEAD.   *(Reading.)*
Do Not Resuscitate.
Kelekian. Shit.

(The Code Team stops working.)

JASON.   *(Whispering.)* Oh, God.

CODE TEAM HEAD.
Order was put in yesterday.

CODE TEAM.
    — It's a doctor fuck-up.
    — What is he, a resident?
    — Got us up here on a
      DNR.
    — Called a code on a
      no-code.
JASON.
Oh, God.
(The bedside scene fades.)

66

PROPERTY LIST

IV pole (VIVIAN, SUSIE)
Papers (KELEKIAN)
Informed consent form (KELEKIAN)
Pen (VIVIAN)
Medical chart (SUSIE, JASON)
Wheelchair (SUSIE, TECHNICIAN, TECHNICIAN 2)
Paraphernalia for taking temperature, pulse and respiration rate
    (SUSIE)
Wheeled stool (JASON)
Sheets of paper (JASON)
Exam gloves (JASON)
Large plastic washbasin (VIVIAN)
Pile of 6 white books (VIVIAN)
Juice with straw (SUSIE)
Washcloth, water (SUSIE)
Surgical masks, gowns and gloves (KELEKIAN, JASON)
Intake and output graphs, on or near bed (JASON)
Commode
Pointer (TECHNICIAN)
2 stick Popsicle (SUSIE)
Morphine (SUSIE)
Catheter (SUSIE)
Baby oil (SUSIE)
Paper bag with children's book (E.M.)
Code Blue equipment (CODE TEAM)

ABOUT THE AUTHOR

Margaret Edson lives in Atlanta, Georgia, where she is an elementary school teacher. Between earning degrees in history and literature, she worked in the cancer and AIDS unit of a research hospital. *Wit* is her first play.

NEW PLAYS

★ **HONOUR by Joanna Murray-Smith.** In a series of intense confrontations, a wife, husband, lover and daughter negotiate the forces of passion, history, responsibility and honour. "HONOUR makes for surprisingly interesting viewing. Tight, crackling dialogue (usually played out in punchy verbal duels) captures characters unable to deal with emotions ... Murray-Smith effectively places her characters in situations that strip away pretense." –*Variety* "... the play's virtues are strong: a distinctive theatrical voice, passionate concerns ... HONOUR might just capture a few honors of its own." –*Time Out Magazine* [1M, 3W] ISBN: 0-8222-1683-3

★ **MR. PETERS' CONNECTIONS by Arthur Miller.** Mr. Miller describes the protagonist as existing in a dream-like state when the mind is "freed to roam from real memories to conjectures, from trivialities to tragic insights, from terror of death to glorying in one's being alive." With this memory play, the Tony Award and Pulitzer Prize-winner reaffirms his stature as the world's foremost dramatist. "... a cross between Joycean stream-of-consciousness and Strindberg's dream plays, sweetened with a dose of William Saroyan's philosophical whimsy ... CONNECTIONS is most intriguing ..." –*The NY Times* [5M, 3W] ISBN: 0-8222-1687-6

★ **THE WAITING ROOM by Lisa Loomer.** Three women from different centuries meet in a doctor's waiting room in this dark comedy about the timeless quest for beauty – and its cost. "... THE WAITING ROOM ... is a bold, risky melange of conflicting elements that is ... terrifically moving ... There's no resisting the fierce emotional pull of the play." –*The NY Times* "... one of the high points of this year's Off-Broadway season ... THE WAITING ROOM is well worth a visit." –*Back Stage* [7M, 4W, flexible casting] ISBN: 0-8222-1594-2

★ **THE OLD SETTLER by John Henry Redwood.** A sweet-natured comedy about two church-going sisters in 1943 Harlem and the handsome young man who rents a room in their apartment. "For all of its decent sentiments, THE OLD SETTLER avoids sentimentality. It has the authenticity and lack of pretense of an Early American sampler." –*The NY Times* "We've had some fine plays Off-Broadway this season, and this is one of the best." –*The NY Post* [1M, 3W] ISBN: 0-8-222-1642-6

★ **THE LAST TRAIN TO NIBROC by Arlene Hutton.** In 1940 two young strangers share a seat on a train bound east only to find their paths will cross again. "All aboard. LAST TRAIN TO NIBROC is a sweetly told little chamber romance." –*Show Business* "... [a] gently charming little play, reminiscent of Thorton Wilder in its look at rustic Americans who are to be treasured for their simplicity and directness ..." –*Associated Press* "The old formula of boy wins girls, boy loses girl, boy wins girl still works ... [a] well-made play that perfectly captures a slice of small-town-life-gone-by." –*Back Stage* [1M, 1W] ISBN: 0-8222-1753-8

★ **OVER THE RIVER AND THROUGH THE WOODS by Joe DiPietro.** Nick sees both sets of his grandparents every Sunday for dinner. This is routine until he has to tell them that he's been offered a dream job in Seattle. The news doesn't sit so well. "A hilarious family comedy that is even funnier than his long running musical revue *I Love You, You're Perfect, Now Change*." –*Back Stage* "Loaded with laughs every step of the way." –*Star-Ledger* [3M, 3W] ISBN: 0-8222-1712-0

★ **SIDE MAN by Warren Leight.** 1999 Tony Award winner. This is the story of a broken family and the decline of jazz as popular entertainment. "... a tender, deeply personal memory play about the turmoil in the family of a jazz musician as his career crumbles at the dawn of the age of rock-and-roll ..." –*The NY Times* "[SIDE MAN] is an elegy for two things – a lost world and a lost love. When the two notes sound together in harmony, it is moving and graceful ..." –*The NY Daily News* "An atmospheric memory play...with crisp dialogue and clearly drawn characters ... reflects the passing of an era with persuasive insight ... The joy and despair of the musicians is skillfully illustrated." –*Variety* [5M, 3W] ISBN: 0-8222-1721-X

DRAMATISTS PLAY SERVICE, INC.
440 Park Avenue South, New York, NY 10016 212-683-8960 Fax 212-213-1539
postmaster@dramatists.com www.dramatists.com

NEW PLAYS

★ **CLOSER by Patrick Marber.** Winner of the 1998 Olivier Award for Best Play and the 1999 New York Drama Critics Circle Award for Best Foreign Play. Four lives intertwine over the course of four and a half years in this densely plotted, stinging look at modern love and betrayal. "CLOSER is a sad, savvy, often funny play that casts a steely, unblinking gaze at the world of relationships and lets you come to your own conclusions ... CLOSER does not merely hold your attention; it burrows into you." –*New York Magazine* "A powerful, darkly funny play about the cosmic collision between the sun of love and the comet of desire." –*Newsweek Magazine* [2M, 2W] ISBN: 0-8222-1722-8

★ **THE MOST FABULOUS STORY EVER TOLD by Paul Rudnick.** A stage manager, headset and prompt book at hand, brings the house lights to half, then dark, and cues the creation of the world. Throughout the play, she's in control of everything. In other words, she's either God, or she thinks she is. "Line by line, Mr. Rudnick may be the funniest writer for the stage in the United States today ... One-liners, epigrams, withering put-downs and flashing repartee: These are the candles that Mr. Rudnick lights instead of cursing the darkness ... a testament to the virtues of laughing ... and in laughter, there is something like the memory of Eden." –*The NY Times* "Funny it is ... consistently, rapaciously, deliriously ... easily the funniest play in town." –*Variety* [4M, 5W] ISBN: 0-8222-1720-1

★ **A DOLL'S HOUSE by Henrik Ibsen, adapted by Frank McGuinness.** Winner of the 1997 Tony Award for Best Revival. "New, raw, gut-twisting and gripping. Easily the hottest drama this season." –*USA Today* "Bold, brilliant and alive." –*The Wall Street Journal* "A thunderclap of an evening that takes your breath away." –*Time Magazine* [4M, 4W, 2 boys] ISBN: 0-8222-1636-1

★ **THE HERBAL BED by Peter Whelan.** The play is based on actual events which occurred in Stratford-upon-Avon in the summer of 1613, when William Shakespeare's elder daughter was publicly accused of having a sexual liaison with a married neighbor and family friend. "In his probing new play, THE HERBAL BED ... Peter Whelan muses about a sidelong event in the life of Shakespeare's family and creates a finely textured tapestry of love and lies in the early 17th-century Stratford." –*The NY Times* "It is a first rate drama with interesting moral issues of truth and expediency." –*The NY Post* [5M, 3W] ISBN: 0-8222-1675-2

★ **SNAKEBIT by David Marshall Grant.** A study of modern friendship when put to the test. "... a rather smart and absorbing evening of water-cooler theater, the intimate sort of Off-Broadway experience that has you picking apart the recognizable characters long after the curtain calls." – *The NY Times* "Off-Broadway keeps on presenting us with compelling reasons for going to the theater. The latest is SNAKEBIT, David Marshall Grant's smart new comic drama about being thirtysomething and losing one's way in life." –*The NY Daily News* [3M, 1W] ISBN: 0-8222-1724-4

★ **A QUESTION OF MERCY by David Rabe.** The Obie Award-winning playwright probes the sensitive and controversial issue of doctor-assisted suicide in the age of AIDS in this poignant drama. "There are many devastating ironies in Mr. Rabe's beautifully considered, piercingly clear-eyed work ..." –*The NY Times* "With unsettling candor and disturbing insight, the play arouses pity and understanding of a troubling subject ... Rabe's provocative tale is an affirmation of dignity that rings clear and true." –*Variety* [6M, 1W] ISBN: 0-8222-1643-4

★ **DIMLY PERCEIVED THREATS TO THE SYSTEM by Jon Klein.** Reality and fantasy overlap with hilarious results as this unforgettable family attempts to survive the nineties. "Here's a play whose point about fractured families goes to the heart, mind – and ears." –*The Washington Post* "... an end-of-the millennium comedy about a family on the verge of a nervous breakdown ... Trenchant and hilarious ..." –*The Baltimore Sun* [2M, 4W] ISBN: 0-8222-1677-9

DRAMATISTS PLAY SERVICE, INC.
440 Park Avenue South, New York, NY 10016 212-683-8960 Fax 212-213-1539
postmaster@dramatists.com www.dramatists.com

NEW PLAYS

★ **AS BEES IN HONEY DROWN by Douglas Carter Beane.** Winner of the John Gassner Playwriting Award. A hot young novelist finds the subject of his new screenplay in a New York socialite who leads him into the world of *Auntie Mame* and *Breakfast at Tiffany's*, before she takes him for a ride. "A delicious soufflé of a satire ... [an] extremely entertaining fable for an age that always chooses image over substance." –*The NY Times* "... A witty assessment of one of the most active and relentless industries in a consumer society ... the creation of 'hot' young things, which the media have learned to mass produce with efficiency and zeal." –*The NY Daily News* [3M, 3W, flexible casting] ISBN: 0-8222-1651-5

★ **STUPID KIDS by John C. Russell.** In rapid, highly stylized scenes, the story follows four high-school students as they make their way from first through eighth period and beyond, struggling with the fears, frustrations, and longings peculiar to youth. "In STUPID KIDS ... playwright John C. Russell gets the opera of adolescence to a T ... The stylized teenspeak of STUPID KIDS ... suggests that Mr. Russell may have hidden a tape recorder under a desk in study hall somewhere and then scoured the tapes for good quotations ... it is the kids' insular, ceaselessly churning world, a pre-adult world of Doritos and libidos, that the playwright seeks to lay bare." –*The NY Times* "STUPID KIDS [is] a sharp-edged ... whoosh of teen angst and conformity anguish. It is also very funny." –*NY Newsday* [2M, 2W] ISBN: 0-8222-1698-1

★ **COLLECTED STORIES by Donald Margulies.** From Obie Award-winner Donald Margulies comes a provocative analysis of a student-teacher relationship that turns sour when the protégé becomes a rival. "With his fine ear for detail, Margulies creates an authentic, insular world, and he gives equal weight to the opposing viewpoints of two formidable characters." –*The LA Times* "This is probably Margulies' best play to date ..." –*The NY Post* "... always fluid and lively, the play is thick with ideas, like a stock-pot of good stew." –*The Village Voice* [2W] ISBN: 0-8222-1640-X

★ **FREEDOMLAND by Amy Freed.** An overdue showdown between a son and his father sets off fireworks that illuminate the neurosis, rage and anxiety of one family – and of America at the turn of the millennium. "FREEDOMLAND's more obvious links are to *Buried Child* and *Bosoms and Neglect*. Freed, like Guare, is an inspired wordsmith with a gift for surreal touches in situations grounded in familiar and real territory." –*Curtain Up* [3M, 4W] ISBN: 0-8222-1719-8

★ **STOP KISS by Diana Son.** A poignant and funny play about the ways, both sudden and slow, that lives can change irrevocably. "There's so much that is vital and exciting about STOP KISS ... you want to embrace this young author and cheer her onto other works ... the writing on display here is funny and credible ... you also will be charmed by its heartfelt characters and up-to-the-minute humor." –*The NY Daily News* "... irresistibly exciting ... a sweet, sad, and enchantingly sincere play." –*The NY Times* [3M, 3W] ISBN: 0-8222-1731-7

★ **THREE DAYS OF RAIN by Richard Greenberg.** The sins of fathers and mothers make for a bittersweet elegy in this poignant and revealing drama. "... a work so perfectly judged it heralds the arrival of a major playwright ... Greenberg is extraordinary." –*The NY Daily News* "Greenberg's play is filled with graceful passages that are by turns melancholy, harrowing, and often, quite funny." –*Variety* [2M, 1W] ISBN: 0-8222-1676-0

★ **THE WEIR by Conor McPherson.** In a bar in rural Ireland, the local men swap spooky stories in an attempt to impress a young woman from Dublin who recently moved into a nearby "haunted" house. However, the tables are soon turned when she spins a yarn of her own. "You shed all sense of time at this beautiful and devious new play." –*The NY Times* "Sheer theatrical magic. I have rarely been so convinced that I have just seen a modern classic. Tremendous." –*The London Daily Telegraph* [4M, 1W] ISBN: 0-8222-1706-6

DRAMATISTS PLAY SERVICE, INC.
440 Park Avenue South, New York, NY 10016 212-683-8960 Fax 212-213-1539
postmaster@dramatists.com www.dramatists.com